My First Sight Words and Sentences

Anjie Chatt

PREFACE

Learning to read and write simple words and sentences can help your child build the foundation of literacy skills. An early grasp of basic reading and writing skills can give the children the confidence boost they need in a classroom environment.

Om Kidz | Om Books International

Reprinted in 2024

Corporate & Editorial Office
A-12, Sector 64, Noida 201 301
Uttar Pradesh, India
Phone: +91 120 477 4100
Email: editorial@ombooks.com
Website: www.ombooksinternational.com

Sales Office
107, Ansari Road, Darya Ganj
New Delhi 110 002, India
Phone: +91 11 4000 9000
Email: sales@ombooks.com

Author: Anjie Chatt

ISBN: 978-93-52769-39-1

Printed in India

10 9 8 7 6 5 4 3 2

CONTENT

ate

Read and tick (✓) the circle.

Audrey ate jam sandwich for breakfast. ◯

Her father ate toast and tea for breakfast. ◯

She ate chicken salad for lunch. ◯

Her mother ate French toast for breakfast. ◯

Her friend, Diana, ate pasta for lunch. 

In the evening, Audrey and
Diana ate ice cream. ◯

For dinner, Audrey ate her favourite food, fish and chips. ◯

Diana ate corn and spinach pie. ◯

'Ate' is a verb.

any

Read and tick (✓) the circle.

Julie did not have any sugar for her tea. ◯

Andy did not have any flour to bake a cake. ◯

Sam did not have any pencils to draw. ◯

Tina did not have any shoelaces for her shoes. ◯

June did not have any coins for the vending machine. ◯

Carrie did not have any eggs left in the refrigerator. ◯

'Any' is a determiner used with uncountable or plural nouns.

again

Read and tick (✓) the circle.

It started raining once again. ◯

Sara packed her bag again after putting in her toothbrush that she had forgotten. ◯

Myra had to do her homework again after she dropped water on the sheets. ◯

Jeremy had to go back home from school again as he had forgotten his books. ◯

Andrea had to wait at the bus stop as the bus was late again. ◯

We could not go home from the office as it had started snowing again. ◯

'Again' is an adverb.

black

Read and tick (✓) the circle.

Lucy is a black dog. ○

Her best friend, Bobby, has black spots on his body. ○

Lucy's mother has black eyes and nose. ○

Lucy and Bobby love to chase their black and white ball. ○

When Lucy goes home, she drinks water from a black bowl. ○

Bobby eats his food in a black bowl too! ○

'Black' is used as an adjective here.

around

Read and tick (✓) the circle.

The car went around the lake. ◯

The tour bus went around the castle. ◯

The train went around the mountains. ◯

Bobby walked all around the palace. ◯

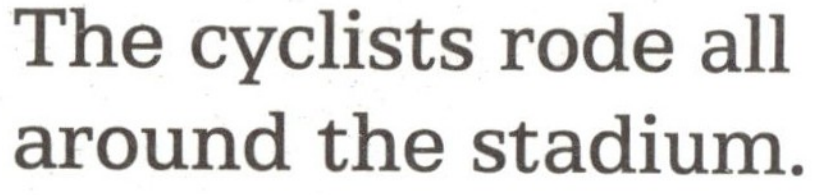

The cyclists rode all around the stadium. ◯

The students played all around the school ground at lunch. ◯

'Around' is a preposition.

because

Read and tick (✓) the circle.

I was late because it was raining. ◯

It was very cold because it had snowed in the evening. ◯

The roads were slippery because there was a hailstorm. ◯

We had to wear windbreakers because it was very windy. ◯

We were stuck at school because the buses were late. ◯

We could fly kites because it was a holiday today! ◯

'Because' is a conjunction joining words or phrases.

been

Read and tick (✓) the circle.

I have been waiting for my coffee to brew.

You have been to the library today.

We have been to this movie theatre last week.

Darren had been to see the dentist today.

Simon had been to the bookstore to buy the latest mystery novel.

I have been waiting for this package to arrive.

'Been' is a verb known as past participle.

before

Read and tick (✓) the circle.

Before I eat, I wash my hands. ◯

Before I go to school, I brush my teeth. ◯

Before I go to play, I wear my favourite sneakers. ◯

Before dinner, I play video games. ◯

Before I sleep, my mother always reads to me. ◯

I brush my teeth before I go to sleep. ◯

'Before' is a preposition.

best

Read and tick (✓) the circle.

Amy said, "It is Cecil's 18th birthday. I want to make it his best birthday ever!" ◯

Victoria said, "I want to wear my best dress to the school dance." ◯

The teacher said, "The best artist will win a visit to the Universal Studios." ◯

Cheryl said, "My car is the best!" ◯

Manny said, "This magic show is the best." ◯

Dawson said, "Rudy is the best reindeer in the whole town." ◯

'Best' is an adjective.

both

Read and tick (✓) the circle.

Both the children were in the same class. ◯

Both the bunnies ran off to the lettuce farm. ◯

Both my parents are doctors. ◯

Both of us will be travelling soon. ◯

Both the boys wanted to eat strawberry ice cream. ◯

Both of us love to go to the movies. ◯

'Both' is a pronoun used with plural nouns to mean two.

buy

Read and tick (✓) the circle.

I want to buy colour pencils. ◯

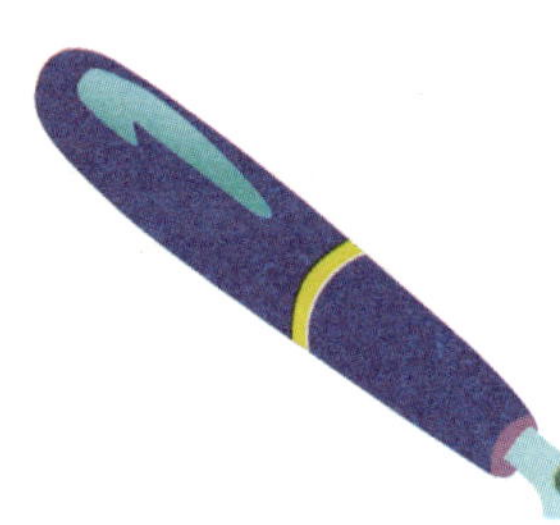

John wants to buy a pen. ◯

Jeff wants to buy a drawing book. ◯

Lily wants to buy a notebook. ◯

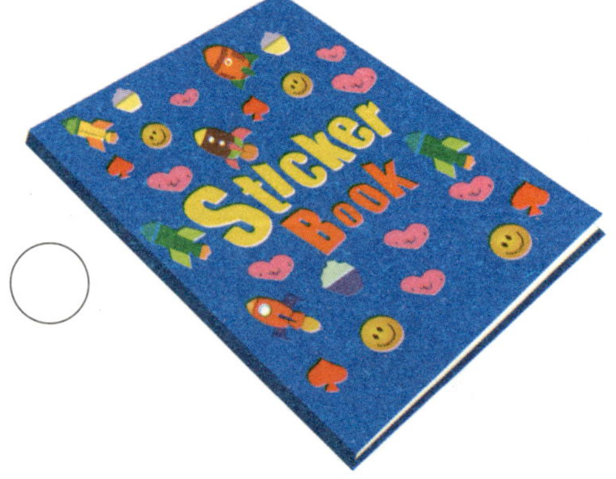

Macy wants to buy a sticker book. ◯

Chris wants to buy origami paper. ◯

'Buy' is a verb.

brown

Read and tick (✓) the circle.

Everywhere I look, I see brown-coloured things. ◯

There is brown bread on my breakfast table. ◯

My favourite fruit kiwi is brown on the outside. ◯

My school trousers are brown in colour and I have a matching brown hat. ◯

My dad says that mountains are often brown in colour and if you look closely you will see a lot of brown buildings in your hometown! ◯

'Brown' is an adjective, a noun and the name of a colour.

called

Read and tick (✓) the circle.

Tina said, "I called Matt and asked if he wanted to play." ◯

Father said to Mother, "I called an ambulance for grandmother." ◯

Holly said to Ron, "I called you a taxi." ◯

The doctor said, "You could have called me at the office." ◯

Dina said, "I called up Kim right away. She might need our help." ◯

The teacher said, "I called Danish's name at roll call today but he was absent." ◯

Cara said, "I called my dentist but he is out of town." ◯

'Called' is the past tense of the verb 'call'.

cold

Read and tick (✓) the circle.

It is very cold today. ◯

Jack refused to get out of bed because it was too cold. ◯

Joey liked the cold and she went for a long walk wearing snow boots. ◯

Mother made a big fire to keep the cold away. ◯

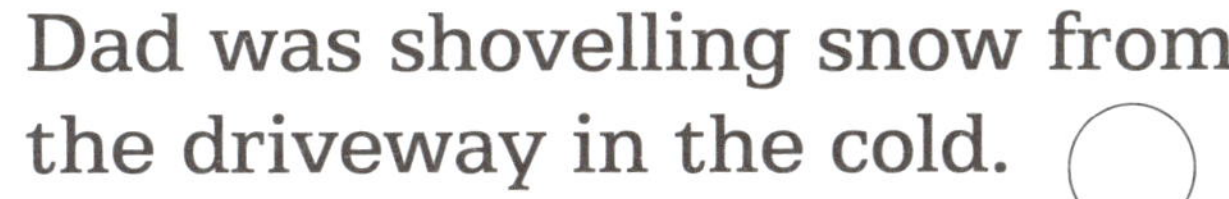

Dad was shovelling snow from the driveway in the cold. ◯

Jack decided the best way to beat the cold was to drink lots of hot chocolate. ◯

'Cold' is an adjective and noun.

could

Read and tick (✓) the circle.

I could not open the door. ◯

Kira could not open it either. ◯

Then father tried, but he could not open it either. ◯

Mother said maybe Hans the locksmith could open the door. ◯

Lo, behold! The door opened! ◯

Everybody clapped. ◯

'Could' is a verb used as the past tense of 'can.'

did

Read and tick (✓) the circle.

I did finish my test just in time. ◯

He did not reach the airport on time to pick up his friend. ◯

Jamie did not wait for the train as it was running late. ◯

Eunice did not find his shirt in the washing machine. ◯

The dog did not find his bone in the hole. ◯

The fox did not find the chickens. ◯

'Did' is the past tense of the verb 'do'.

does

Read and tick (✓) the circle.

Does Doug know you? ◯

Does your dog bite? ◯

Does Henry play the piano? ◯

When does the bus arrive? ◯

Does Paul like oranges or apples? ◯

How long does it take to reach the beach? ◯

'Does' is a form of the action word 'do.'

Don't

Read and tick (✓) the circle.

Kelly said, "Don't ask me any questions now. I am very busy." ◯

Charlie said to Matt, "Don't cry. I will buy you another toy." ◯

The teacher said to the class, "Don't talk!" ◯

Derek said, "Don't give up. We are very close to the top of the mountain." ◯

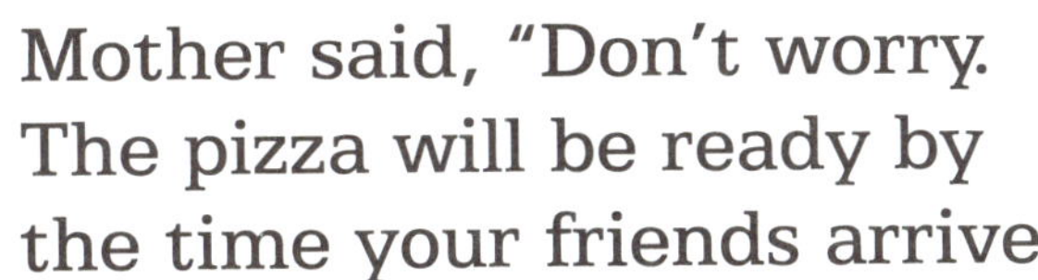

Mother said, "Don't worry. The pizza will be ready by the time your friends arrive." ◯

Father yelled, "Don't touch the spider. It can bite!" ◯

Tammy said, "I don't mind waiting for the train." ◯

'Don't' is the short form of 'do not'.

eat

Read and tick (✓) the circle.

The children were very hungry after their basketball game. ◯

Jana said, "I want to eat a big pizza!" ◯

Shawn said, "Let us eat some healthy food. How about a mixed vegetarian salad?" ◯

Jana said, "I could eat a salad, a roasted chicken and some cheesecake as well." ◯

Shawn said, "It sounds like you could eat a horse!" ◯

Jana said, "I want to eat dessert too. Would you like to eat some strawberry ice cream?" ◯

Shawn said, 'I would love to eat strawberry ice cream!" ◯

'Eat' is a verb.

every

Read and tick (✓) the circle.

Every day the Sun rises from the east. ◯

Every day the Sun sets in the west. 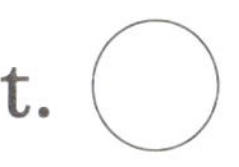

I go to school every day. ◯

I play in the park with my friend every day. ◯

I watch television every day too! ◯

I like eating dinner with my parents and sister every day. ◯

'Every' is an adjective used before countable noun.

Practice Sheet I

Find and circle the sight words that you have just learnt.

before

cold

around

black

called

ate

does

been

best
buy
don't
did
because
eat
both
brown
could

fast

Read and tick (✓) the circle.

Mr Squirrel drives a fast car. ◯

It is pink in colour and has a cool rear view mirror. ◯

One day, while Mr Squirrel was driving his car, really fast down the lane, another car honked very loudly from behind. ◯

He looked back and saw a fellow squirrel dressed rather smartly in a waist coat and red bow, driving a big blue car, really fast down the lane. ◯

Before he knew it, the blue car overtook him and went racing down the valley very fast. ◯

Mr Squirrel started driving fast too but the blue car was long gone! ◯

'Fast' is an adjective and an adverb.

found

Read and tick (✓) the circle.

I found a penny under my bed! ◯

Julius found his English book in the car. ◯

Paris found her lost puppy in the garage. ◯

Hilda found the riverside to be very quiet. ◯

Drake found his cat hiding under his bed. ◯

Timothy found his car in the lake! ◯

'Found' is a verb.

four

Read and tick (✓) the circle.

There are four people in Jen's family. ◯

There are four cows crossing the road. ◯

There are four masks hanging on the wall. ◯

We need four more chairs in the garden. ◯

There are four puppies in this basket. ◯

There are four pigeons sitting on a branch. ◯

'Four' is a noun. It is a number name.

give

Read and tick (✓) the circle.

It was Mother's birthday. ◯

Laila wanted to give her a necklace as a present. ◯

Bryan could not think of anything special to give her. ◯

Father said, "Bryan, what is the one thing that makes Mother happy?" ◯

Bryan thought for a while and said, "Flowers. She always likes to give flowers from her garden to her friends. ◯

Father said, "Maybe you can buy her some beautiful flowers and give them to her for her birthday." ◯

Mother loved the flowers and necklace! ◯

'Give' is a verb.

going

Read and tick (✓) the circle.

Pablo, Alicia, Robert, Mia and Serena were going to the zoo. ◯

Pablo was going to see the polar bears. ◯

Alicia loved elephants and she was going to see the elephant show! ◯

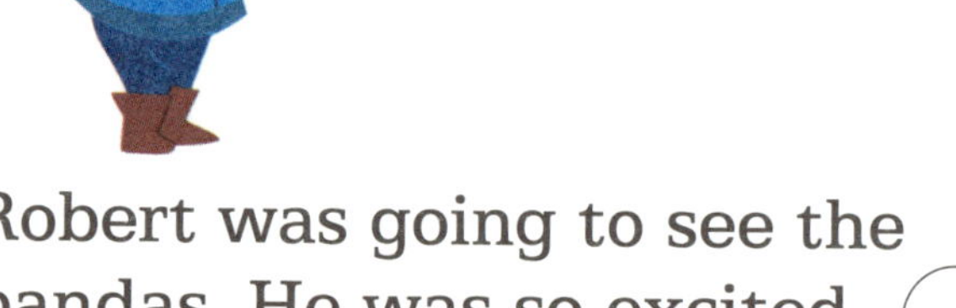

Robert was going to see the pandas. He was so excited. ◯

Mia and Serena were going to see the white tigers. ◯

It was going to be an exciting day. ◯

'Going' is a verb that is a continuous form of 'go'.

good

Read and tick (✓) the circle.

The weather is good today. ○

The breakfast at this hotel is good. ○

We had a good walk along the river. ○

This dark chocolate is good, but that chocolate is too sweet. ○

This book is good but the movie is not as good. ○

The dessert which Mother made was really good. I ate too much! ○

'Good' is an adjective.

how

Read and tick (✓) the circle.

Peter said, "I know how to ski." ◯

Elizabeth asked her mother, "How is your cold?" ◯

Beth asked, "How about we meet in front of the Union Station?" ◯

Lisa asked Tim, "How was your day?" ◯

The doctor asked the nurse, "How is Mr Hunt feeling today?" ◯

Tyron asked the little boy, "How did you find my house?" ◯

'How' is an adverb.

into

Read and tick (✓) the circle.

The mouse ran into a hole. ○

The cat tried to get into the hole. ○

The hole was too small and the cat's paw went half way into it and got stuck! ○

Then, the mouse ran out of the hole and hid behind the bathtub. ○

The cat finally got out of the hole and ran into the bathroom looking for the mouse. ○

The mouse jumped out of the window and into the flower pot below it. ○

The cat jumped after the mouse and fell into a tub of hot water. He ran off in a fright! ○

The mouse ran back into his hole and laughed. ○

'Into" is a preposition.

its

Read and tick (✓) the circle.

My dog sleeps in its kennel at night. ◯

Aria's cat has its own pink bed. ◯

Maria's horse ate its carrots happily. ◯

Paris is known for its beauty. ◯

Gabrielle found and returned the kitten to its owner. ◯

A snake sheds its skin. ◯

'Its' is a determiner.

just

Read and tick (✓) the circle.

I just called my grandmother. ◯

We just finished eating dinner. ◯

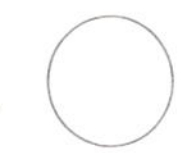

Tara just dropped in to see her best friend. ◯

The airplane just landed. ◯

Jackson had just turned the television on when there was a knock on his door. ◯

Isabella just arrived in England from Italy. ◯

'Just' is an adverb.

know

Read and tick (✓) the circle.

I know I want to be a pilot when I grow up. ○

I know Rob wants to be an astronaut. ○

I know Jay wants to be a formula race car driver. ○

I know Andy wants to be a painter. ○

I know Elliot wants to be a scientist. ○

I know Kevin wants to be an actor. ○

'Know' is a verb.

let

Read and tick (✓) the circle.

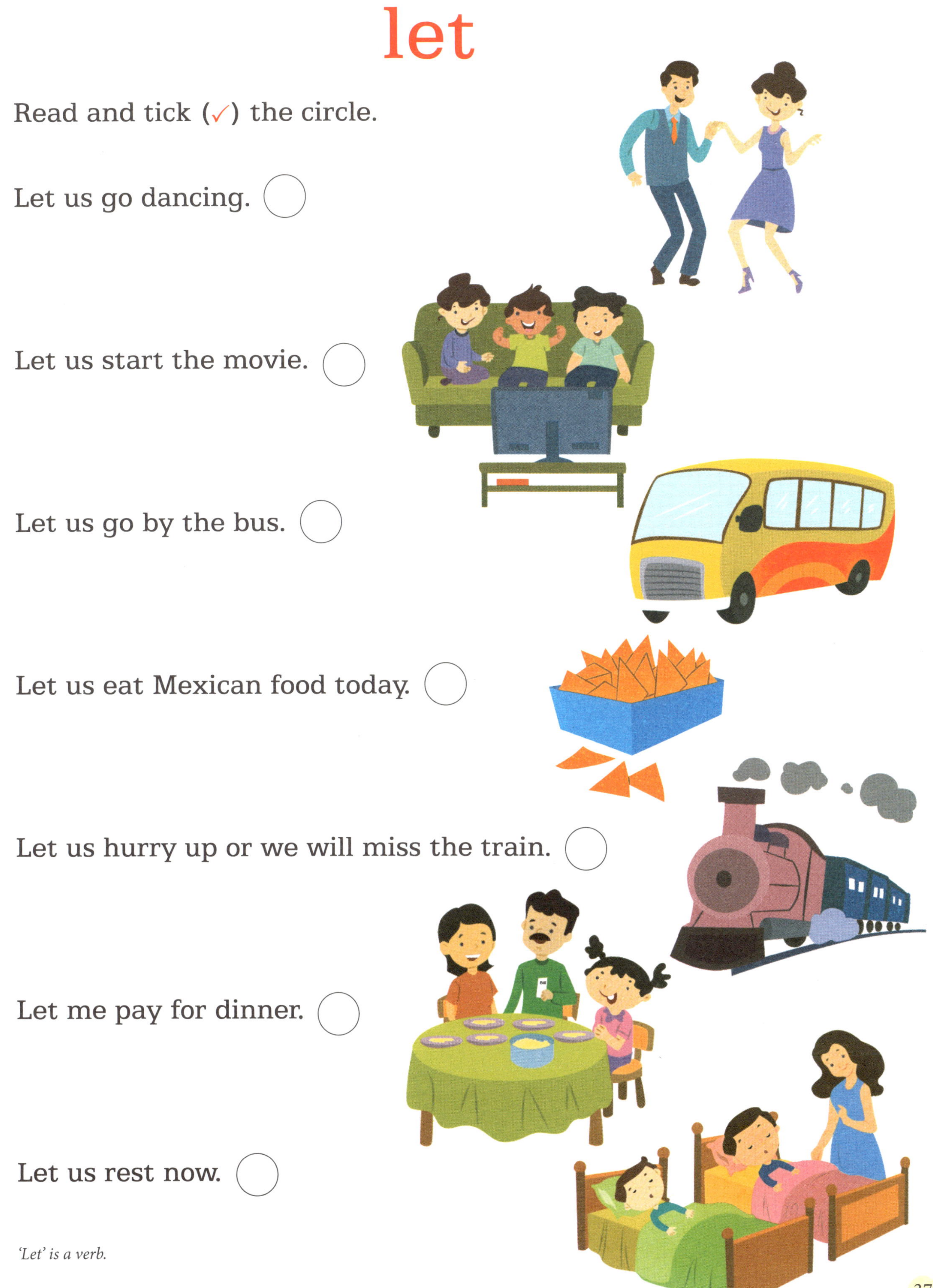

Let us go dancing. ◯

Let us start the movie. ◯

Let us go by the bus. ◯

Let us eat Mexican food today. ◯

Let us hurry up or we will miss the train. ◯

Let me pay for dinner. ◯

Let us rest now. ◯

'Let' is a verb.

must

Read and tick (✓) the circle.

He must leave now. ◯

We must finish decorating this room by noon. ◯

She must go to see her sick brother soon. ◯

I must have lost my necklace on the bus. ◯

Gina must be tired after working all night. ◯

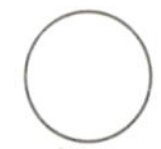

Phoebe must buy a new pair of shoes. ◯

'Must' is a helping or modal verb.

new

Read and tick (✓) the circle.

Sara and her family moved into a new house. ◯

The sofa was all new. ◯

The pots and pans were all new. ◯

The carpet was new. ◯

The cupboard was new. ◯

The curtains were new as well. ◯

Sara and her family loved their new home! ◯

'New' is an adjective.

number

Read and tick (✓) the circle.

Do you know that every number has a name? Let us read the number names.

○	twenty one	○	thirty one
○	twenty two	○	thirty two
○	twenty three	○	thirty three
○	twenty four	○	thirty four
○	twenty five	○	thirty five
○	twenty six	○	thirty six
○	twenty seven	○	thirty seven
○	twenty eight	○	thirty eight
○	twenty nine	○	thirty nine
○	thirty	○	forty

once

Read and tick (✓) the circle.

Once I went fishing with my father. ◯

It was at once, an exciting and tiring trip. ◯

We travelled almost 100 miles west to a huge lake. Once we reached there, I felt tired already! ◯

It was still dark. Once the Sun came up, we set up our fishing rods. ◯

I held my rod and at once I felt something pull at the rod. But it was just a plastic bag that was stuck to my hook. ◯

Then a very big fish got caught in my Dad's rod and began pulling at the line. But once my dad reeled in the fish, it stopped pulling. I was very excited. It was a huge haddock! ◯

Once again, I felt that this was great fun and we should do it more often. ◯

'Once' is an adverb.

Practice Sheet II

Find and circle the Sight Words that you have just learnt.

found
just
four
let
number
once
fast
gives

please

Read and tick (✓) the circle.

I would like to buy this book, please. ◯

Please turn off the lights when you leave the room. ◯

Please submit your essays by Friday. ◯

Please be kind to animals. ◯

Please bring some snacks to the party. ◯

Please drive carefully. ◯

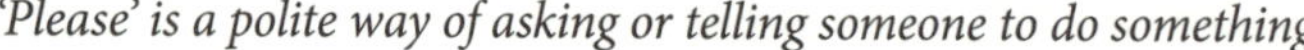

'Please' is a polite way of asking or telling someone to do something.

pretty

Read and tick (✓) the circle.

The world is full of pretty things. ◯

There are many pretty flowers on Earth. ◯

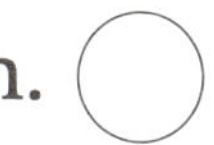

There are many pretty trees, too! ◯

There are pretty lakes as well. ◯

Then, there are pretty animals like the peacock! ◯

But the most pretty thing is friendship! ◯

'Pretty' is an adjective.

ran

Read and tick (✓) the circle.

The squirrel ran up the tree. ◯

The tiger ran after the deer. ◯

The fox ran after the snake. ◯

The dog ran after the cat. ◯

The cat ran after the mouse. ◯

The mouse ran up the clock. 

'Ran' is an action word.

ride

Read and tick (✓) the circle.

Jenna wanted to ride on a horse. ◯

She went to a riding school to learn how to ride. ◯

There were other children who came to ride at the school. ◯

Jenna learnt to ride slowly with the other children. ◯

She wanted to ride on the horse very fast. ◯

But the horse was not ready and Jenna fell off when she tried to ride too fast. ◯

Luckily, she was not hurt but she did not ride too fast anymore. ◯

'Ride' is an action word.

so

Read and tick (✓) the circle.

The fruits look so delicious. ◯

The apples are so sweet. ◯

The grapes are so sour. ◯

The banana is so soft. ◯

The sugarcane is so juicy. ◯

The watermelon is so crunchy. ◯

The strawberries are so tart. ◯

'So' is an adverb.

soon

Read and tick (✓) the circle.

The taxi will be here soon.

Terrence will be leaving for practice soon.

Dolly will be coming on stage soon.

My singing lessons start soon.

The rains came too soon.

The children wanted school to be over soon! 

'Soon' is an adverb.

stop

Read and tick (✓) the circle.

The bus came to a stop in front of the station. ◯

We must stop eating too much candy. ◯

My neighbour would stop by to see us every day. ◯

The newspaper boy would never stop to talk! ◯

The ice cream man would stop in front of the school. ◯

The traffic police tried to stop the car. ◯

'Stop' is a verb.

take

Read and tick (✓) the circle.

I wanted to take some snacks to school. ◯

Reggie wanted to take his friend home for dinner. ◯

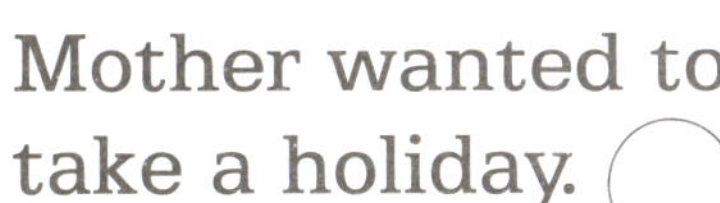

Mother wanted to take a holiday. ◯

Father wanted to take a nap. ◯

Archie wanted to take karate lessons. ◯

Charlene wanted to take singing lessons. ◯

'Take' is a verb.

think

Read and tick (✓) the circle.

Misha said, "I think this dress is lovely." ◯

Bob said, "I think I understand this sum now." ◯

Rex said, "Few people think exercise is fun." ◯

Mandy said, "Do you think I can win this competition? ◯

The teacher said, "Please think about who your favourite movie hero is." ◯

Garry said, "I think Mr Harris is a kind old man." ◯

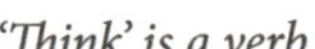

'Think' is a verb.

too

Read and tick (✓) the circle.

I am too tired to run. ◯

The teddy bear is too big. ◯

The music is too loud. ◯

This packet is too big. ◯

Shirley said, "We ate too much." ◯

Mother said to Mimi, "Don't work too hard." ◯

Petra asked, "Is Raffy coming for the soccer match too?" ◯

'Too' is an adverb.

wrote

Read and tick (✓) the circle.

The teacher wrote on both sides of the paper." ◯

Mathias said, "I wrote a poem." 

Judy said, "I wrote a mystery novel." ◯

Ricky said, "I wrote a funny story." ◯

Piers said, "I wrote about my grandmother." ◯

Laura said, "I wrote about my cat."

The teacher said, "You all wrote very good stories." ◯

'Wrote' is the past tense of the verb 'write'.

Activity Time

1. **Read the sentences and write them.**

Read it	**Write it**
I like to eat.	________________________________
Please close the door.	________________________________
I have been here before.	________________________________
My dog is black.	________________________________
The water is brown.	________________________________
I could ride every day.	________________________________

2. Read the sentences and write them.

Read it	Write it
I found a penny.	
He gave his book to me.	
The movie was good.	
The station is too far.	
Before I left home, I switched off the lights.	

3. Read the sentences and write them.

Read it	Write it
We did puzzles today.	
I love to ride horses.	
The flowers are pretty.	
When will the zoo open?	
She ran very fast.	

4. Read the sentences and write them.

Read it	Write it
I know very little about coins.	
He could not find any eggs in the fridge.	
When we left home, it was raining.	
I will call her soon.	
I wrote a novel.	

5. Circle the verbs.

ate	black	brown
please	ride	pretty
ran	cold	gives
found	been	before
going	let	does

6. Match the sight words to the correct objects.

eat	car
four	come
every	flowers
black	mother
brown	weather
found	kiwi
cold	penny
call	cat
pretty	day
please	pigeons
fast	cake

Answers: eat cake, four pigeons, every day, black cat, brown kiwi, found penny, cold weather, pretty flowers, please come, fast car

7. Correct the spellings of these sight words.

aet	___________	ceon	___________
oot	___________	deir	___________
yerev	___________	neeb	___________
dolc	___________	wbron	___________
kacbl	___________	uofr	___________
tasf	___________	opst	___________
causebe	___________	toin	___________
ldcou	___________	nfoud	___________
nar	___________	wrtoe	___________

Answer: ate, too, every, cold, black, fast, because, could, ran, once, ride, been, brown, four, stop, into, found, wrote

Activity Time

8. Correct the spellings of those sight words

thbo	________	vige	________
dah	________	ekta	________
ceon	________	tel	________
wnok	________	yan	________
tusj	________	gaina	________
opst	________	woh	________
nehw	________	rounda	________
yub	________	idd	________

Answer: both, had, once, know, just, stop, when, buy, give, take, let, any, again, how, around, did

9. Write your 10 favourite verbs here.

____

____

____

____

____

____

____

____

____

____

10. **Write your 10 favourite sight words here.**

____

____

____

____

____

____

____

____

____

____